Getting to Know & Love Prophet Muhammad

Peace Be Upon Him

Prophet Muhammad's Biography from Birth to Death

BY THE SINCERE SEEKER **KIDS** COLLECTION

God Sends Messengers & Prophets to Us & Why We Learn About Prophet Muhammad PBUH

Due to God's Love and Mercy, he sent many Messengers and Prophets to teach us about Himself and His religion. God's Messengers and Prophets taught us our life purpose and showed us the way to God. They all taught the same general message that no one should be worshipped except Allah, the Creator of the Heavens and Earth, the Creator of the Universe, the Creator of you and me. The Messengers and Prophets of God taught their people that Allah is the One and Only God, without any partner, son, daughter, or equal. All other gods are false and only the creations of God and not the actual Creator Himself.

The Messengers and Prophet's message came with good news and a warning. The good news is for those who believe in God, obey Him, and live a good, righteous life, letting them know that their past sins will be forgiven and a generous reward of Paradise will be awarded to them in the afterlife in which they will live forever. The warning is for those who disbelieve in God and live a life of disobedience, letting them know that if they continue their evil ways, they will live a bad life in this world and the afterlife.

Studying the life of Prophet Muhammad PBUH is important for many reasons. Studying the life of Prophet Muhammad PBUH is a responsibility given to us by our Creator. It is a form of worship, and we get rewarded for it. The best way to develop and increase our love for him is to study the life of Prophet Muhammad PBUH. Prophet Muhammad PBUH is the perfect role model who showed and taught us the best way to live life and had the best character one could have. We learn about him, so we can follow and copy him to be better humans and get closer to Allah. Studying the Life of Prophet Muhammad PBUH helps us better understand the Holy Quran and its context. Studying Seerah, the life of our Final Prophet, also raises our hopes and gives us optimism.

The Land of Makkah Filled with Idols and Idol Worship

Prophet Muhammad PBUH was born in Mecca in the year of the Elephant. Mecca is the home of the Kaaba, the first house of worship built on Earth by Prophet Abraham and his son Ismael, peace be upon them. Before Prophet Muhammad became a prophet, many people of Mecca worshipped idols. They believed that idols had the power to intercede for them. It was a time full of ignorance, foolishness, and misguidance. At the time, Arabia was a backward nation that did not have monuments, a unified government, or law and order. They also did not have written literature, and many did not know how to read and write. Sadly, they had turned the Kaaba, which was dedicated and built for the service of the One True God, Allah, the Glorious, into a place of worship of idols.

Angel Gabriel Splits Open Prophet Muhammad's Chest & Washes His Heart

Prophet Muhammad's father died before Prophet Muhammad PBUH was born, and he was raised by his mother. At the time, it was a custom for Arabs living in towns to send their young boys to the desert to live with a wet nurse and a Bedouin tribe for a few years, so they could grow stronger and healthier in the harsh climate and for other reasons. As a child, no one initially wanted to take Prophet Muhammad PBUH because he was an orphan, and they wouldn't have gotten much money from him. Then Prophet Muhammad's mother, Aminah, eventually sent her child to live with a poor lady named Halima and her husband to spend a couple of years in the desert. As soon as they had brought Prophet Muhammad PBUH, as a child, they began to see miracles around them. Their old goat that stopped producing milk a while back started to produce it again, and their camel, which was weak and slow, gained strength and speed.

While prophet Muhammad PBUH was out playing with his foster brothers, Angel Gabriel came down in a human form. The other kids saw him and ran screaming in terror to Halima and her husband, thinking Prophet Muhammad PBUH was being abducted. Angel Gabriel forced him to the ground as Prophet Muhammad PBUH struggled to get loose. Angel Gabriel pulled out a golden utensil with a golden tray filled with Zam-Zam Water and began to split open his chest and take out his heart to wash it. Angel Gabriel took out a black blood clot and threw it away, saying, '*this is Shaytan's (Devil) portion.*' He then stitched him back up.

Halima and her husband rushed over to Prophet Muhammad PBUH, whose face was pale from fear. Halimah's husband comforted him with a hug and took him in to rest. They realized something special about this boy and decided it was best to return him to his mother, Aminah, in Mecca. He lived with her for a short period, and then sadly, she passed away from illness on her way back from the city of Yathrib, later called Medina.

His loving grandfather, Abdul Muttalib, raised him for two years. He loved Prophet Muhammad PBUH more than he loved his own children. Prophet Muhammad PBUH would watch and learn from his grandfather what it would be like to be the leader of the Arabs as his grandfather was the senior statemen of their tribe. At the age of 8, Prophet Muhammad's grandfather passed away, and the charge of Prophet Muhammad was passed down to his uncle Abu Talib. The latter was the brother of Prophet Muhammad's father. His uncle also loved and preferred him over his own children. Being an orphan taught Prophet Muhammad PBUH wisdom and helped him mature quickly. He learned to be independent, which helped prepare him to bear the challenging life and battles he would later undergo.

Prophet Muhammad's Marriage to His Wife, Khadijah, Peace be Upon Her

As a young man, Prophet Muhammad PBUH worked as a shepherd for the people of Mecca, bringing him a small wage just like past Prophets, who were shepherds in their time. Prophet Muhammad PBUH did not grow up as many others did, drinking alcohol and consuming other harmful things for the soul or body, nor did he ever worship idols. He established a reputation for himself as an honest and trustworthy person. In his early twenties, due to his maturity and character, he was invited to participate in the Tribe's State meetings with the leaders of the tribe.

Khadijah, peace be upon her, was the wealthiest businesswoman in Makkah. She was known for her pureness, nobility, wisdom, and fortune. She inherited a lot of money from her husband, who had passed away. Her sister had a herd of camels and hired Prophet Muhammad PBUH. Khadijah heard her sister praise Prophet Muhammad PBUH for his nobility, integrity, kindness, good manners, shyness, and other qualities.

Since Khadijah, peace be upon her, was a lady, she could not participate in transactions and trades in person and, instead, invested in business partnerships in Syria and Yemen by sending men to go on her behalf and pay them a fraction of the profits. However, she would often receive fewer profits than she should have because the men she hired would pocket some of them. She decided to employ Prophet Muhammad PBUH to take her merchandise to Syria, even though he was inexperienced. Before accepting the job, he asked his uncle for permission; his uncle said yes. When Prophet Muhammad PBUH returned to Makkah, she noticed triple the profits and blessings she used to get. She was very impressed with his character and dealings. He was known to his community as 'the truthful, the trustworthy.' He was trusted by everyone in the community, even those who did not like him.

Khadijah, peace be upon her, was twice widowed, and many men from her tribe had proposed marriage. Yet, she did not accept any or entertained the thought of getting married. Khadijah's older friend approached Prophet Muhammad PBUH and hinted that Khadijah was interested in marrying him. Khadijah was older than Prophet Muhammad PBUH, and Prophet Muhammad was around 25 years old. Prophet Muhammad PBUH was interested in marrying Khadijah, so he asked permission from his uncle, who thought it was a good idea because of the type of person Khadijah was. They had a beautiful marriage full of love and understanding. Khadijah supported Prophet Muhammad PBUH through his tough years. They had six children together: three sons and three daughters. All the males died in childhood.

Rebuilding of the Kaaba After the Flood

At the age of 35, a flood destroyed the Kaaba, and it needed to be rebuilt. Each tribe in Mecca was responsible for rebuilding a part of the Kaaba. The Black Stone, a holy, sacred object sent down from Paradise within the Kaaba, was removed for the renovation and had to be placed back into it. The leaders of Mecca were in disagreement for five days, and blood was almost shed in trying to determine which clan would have the honor of placing the Black Stone back in its original place. They concluded that the next man who walked in would choose who would put the Black Stone back into its original location.

That person turned out to be Prophet Muhammad PBUH. Instead of choosing a particular person or clan, Prophet Muhammad PBUH asked for a cloth to place the Black Stone in the center and had the leader of each clan hold a corner of the fabric and carry it back to the Kaaba together. Then Prophet Muhammad PBUH set the Back Stone with his two hands in its original place, and all clans were satisfied. This demonstrated and symbolized the future of Prophet Muhammad PBUH and how he would soon unify the Arab tribes under one banner of Islam and unify the religion of Prophet Abraham PBUH after it was destroyed.

Angel Gabriel Comes Down to Prophet Muhammad to Reveal the First Verses of the Quran

As Prophet Muhammad PBUH would walk, he would hear rocks and stones greet him. Prophet Muhammad PBUH would also have pleasant dreams that proved true when he awoke. Prophet Muhammad PBUH had the habit of sitting by himself in a cave called Hira because he felt something was missing in his life, and he didn't know what it was. Even though he had a good wife and children, a good life, and good status in society, he felt something was missing. He knew that having these alone does not bring happiness and contentment. He would go to Cave Hira to think about life, this Universe, and this world. He would meditate, ponder, reflect deeply, and wonder how to worship his Creator.

When Prophet Muhammad PBUH was 40 years old, during Ramadan, Angel Gabriel startled Prophet Muhammad PBUH in the cave and demanded he read, even though he did not know how to read or write. Prophet Muhammad PBUH replied, *'I do not know how to read.'* Angel Gabriel repeated the request twice, and Prophet Muhammad had the same response. Then Angel Gabriel squeezed Prophet Muhammad PBUH so tight that it caused him to lose all his energy. Angel Gabriel grasped Prophet Muhammad PBUH with overwhelming force, then rereleased him. Then the first Recitation of the Holy Quran was revealed to Prophet Muhammad PBUH via Angel Gabriel; *'Recite in the name of your Lord who created man from a clinging substance. Recite, and your Lord is the Most Generous who taught by the pen. Taught man that which he knew not'* (Quran 96:1-5). It was the beginning of Allah, the Glorious first Revelation sent via the Angel Gabriel to humanity meant until the end of times.

Prophet Muhammad PBUH hurried home to his supportive wife in fear and asked her to cover him. She quickly covered him with a cloak. When Prophet Muhammad PBUH had calmed a bit, he told her what had happened and that he was scared. She replied, comforting her husband with the following statement, *'God will never humiliate you, as you are good to your family, you take on other people's burden, and help the needy!'*

Prophet Muhammad PBUH continued to receive Revelations for the remainder of his life. These Revelations were memorized and written down by the Prophet's companions. They were later compiled to make up the Holy Quran we have today.

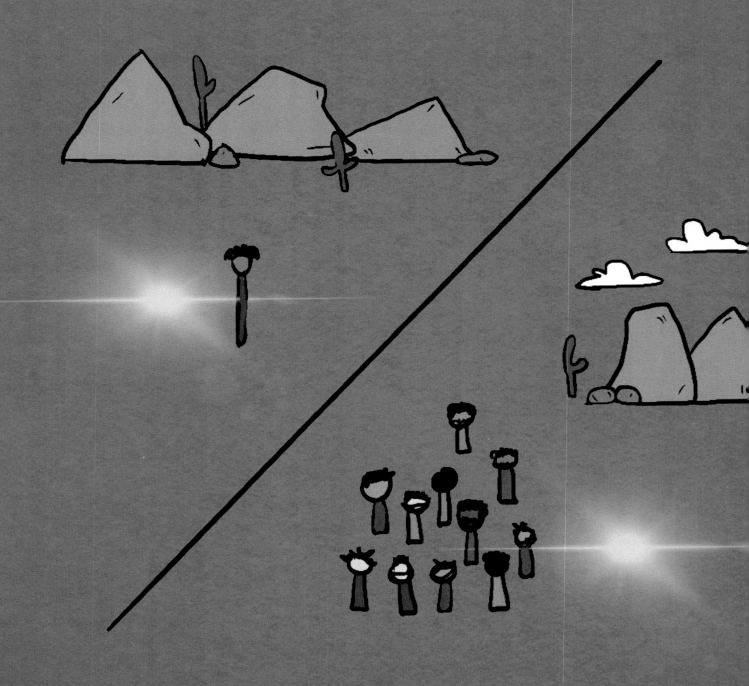

Prophet Muhammad Spreads & Preaches Islam Privately, Then Publicly

Prophet Muhammad PBUH was walking and heard a sound, so he looked up in the Heavens and saw Angel Gabriel sitting on a throne in the Heavens and Earth. Prophet Muhammad PBUH was terrified again and hurried home to his wife and asked her to cover him. Then Angel Gabriel revealed the second Revelation of the Holy Quran: *"O, you who covers himself [with a garment], Arise and warn, And your Lord glorify, And your clothing purify, And uncleanliness avoid, And do not confer favor to acquire more, But for your Lord be patient"* (Quran 74:1-7).

For the first three years, Prophet Muhammad PBUH started to spread the message of Islam privately to his close family and friends, thus freeing them from the practices of their forefathers and the worship of false gods, but he did not publicize the message yet. Prophet Muhammad PBUH taught and preached that there is only one true God that deserves to be worshipped and praised, and all other gods, including idols, are false and are only creations of God, not the actual Creator Himself.

The first person to accept the message of Islam was his wife Khadija and her cousin Waraqah. The first slave to convert was Zaid. The first child to convert was his cousin Ali bin Abi Talib, and the first free adult to convert was his best friend, Abu Bakr As-Siddiq, peace be upon them all.

After three years of secretly struggling to spread Islam to his close companions, Prophet Muhammad PBUH converted 30 people. Then God instructed Prophet Muhammad PBUH to publicize and spread the message of Islam and speak out against idolatry and the worship of false gods to the people of Mecca, then later to spread the message beyond Mecca. Khadijah, peace be upon her, supported the rise of Islam with her wealth by providing food, water, and medicine for the Muslims.

The Idol-Worshippers of Mecca Persecute and Harass the Believers

Prophet Muhammad and his early followers, peace be upon them, were being mistreated, bullied, and harassed by the idol worshippers of their tribe, the Quraishi tribe in Mecca. The idol-worshippers would shame them, mock them, and ridicule them. They would call Prophet Muhammad PBUH a madman, a liar, a sorcerer, a magician, and one possessed by a Jinn. They would prevent Prophet Muhammad PBUH and the Muslims from praying at Allah's Sacred House, the Kaaba, and they would cover them in dirt and filth when praying.

Despite all the ridicule, Prophet Muhammad PBUH continued to gently preach and teach the message of Islam to the Arabs of Mecca. He warned them that if they continued to worship other gods besides Allah and not follow his path, they would face severe punishment like the previous nations who also disobeyed Allah and His Messengers.

The idol-worshippers of Mecca told Prophet Muhammad PBUH if you are really a Prophet of God, why don't you split the moon in half, proving you are a Prophet? Prophet Muhammad PBUH responded if I do this by the will of God, will you then believe I am a Prophet? They answered, yes! Prophet Muhammad PBUH then pointed to the moon, and the moon split in half in front of their eyes. However, Mecca's idol worshippers arrogantly turned around, saying that he'd blinded them to the truth and had bewitched their eyes.

The people of Quraish plotted to stop the Muslims from growing because they worried their power and prestige were at risk, so they made plans to stop them. They tortured the family members that accepted Islam as their religion and way of life. When the harassment by their own people of Quraish grew more severe and unbearable, some Muslims decided to travel to Abyssinia (Ethiopia) to seek shelter and protection in the Kingdom of the Christian King of Abyssinia. He was a fair and righteous king who welcomed the Muslims. This was known as the first Hijrah (Migration) of the Muslims. Later, more Muslims who were being harassed would join them.

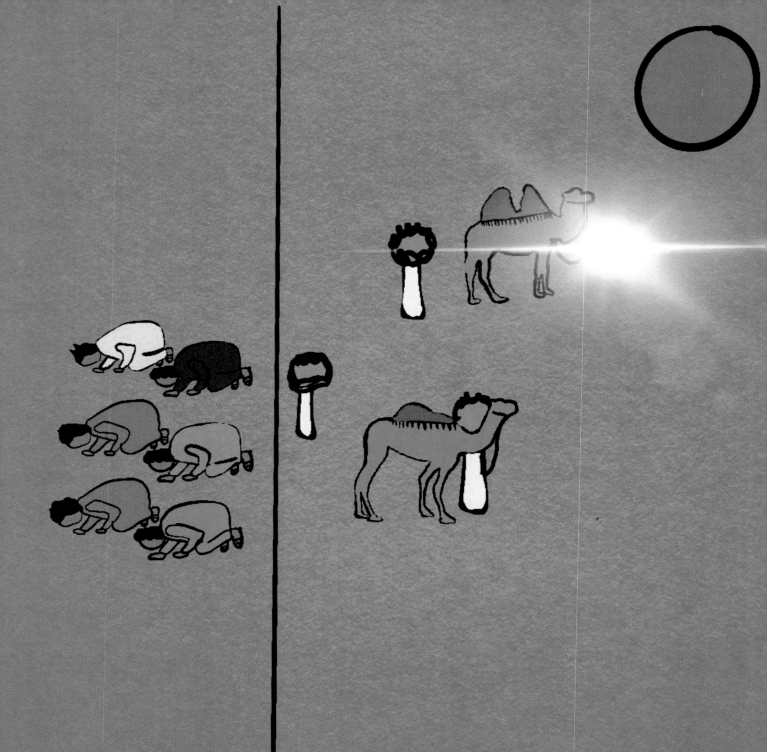

The Idol-Worshippers of Mecca Prostrate to Allah

In Ramadan, Prophet Muhammad PBUH recited Surah An-Najm (The Chapter of the Star) from the Holy Quran to a gathering that included some of the high-ranked idol-worshippers from the Tribe of Quraish in Mecca. The powerful words of Allah impacted the listeners' hearts, and the unbelievers were emotionally overwhelmed. They could not help themselves but unconsciously bowed down in prostration. The idol-worshippers, not present, got upset when they heard what happened. The idol worshippers that prostrated made up lies about what happened to justify why they prostrated.

News of this incident was highly exaggerated and misreported to the Muslims who had migrated to Abyssinia, which led them to think that the idol-worshippers of Mecca had accepted Islam. Hence, they made their way back to Mecca. As the Muslims got close to Mecca, they discovered this rumor was not true. When they arrived at Makkah, some Muslims traveled back to Abyssinia.

With the number of Muslims growing and some big names converting to Islam, this scared the idol worshippers of Makkah. After many attempts to stop Prophet Muhammad PBUH and the believers from spreading Islam, they returned to their old ways of bullying and torturing the Muslims more brutally than they had the first time. The idol-worshippers of Makkah held a meeting and decided not to involve any Muslims in intermarriage or have any business dealings with any of them.

The Year of the Sorrow

In the following year, back-to-back to back calamities hit Prophet Muhammad PBUH within two months. Prophet Muhammad's beloved uncle Abu Talib, who had been protecting him against his enemies, felt sick and died without accepting Islam. About forty days after that, the Prophet's wife, Khadijah, peace be upon her, who was a massive support for him, died as well. It was known as the year of the sorrow, a very tough and sad year for the Prophet PBUH. Prophet Muhammad PBUH was not seen smiling for months.

Later, Prophet Muhammad PBUH and his adopted son, Zaid, traveled to a town called Taif to spread the message of Islam and find protection and support from another city, only to receive disrespect and refusal. They also pelted them with stones, leaving them bloody, and then asked them to return to Mecca. It was Prophet Muhammad's most challenging day of his life.

Prophet Muhammad PBUH needed to migrate to another city for protection. He was secretly reaching out to different tribes on the outskirts of Mecca to spread the message of Allah and find a tribe that would welcome him in their land and support him. Prophet Muhammad PBUH approached five people from the city of Yathrib (later called Medina). He conveyed the message of God to them. They returned to their city and spread the news among their people that a prophet had arisen among the Arabs, who was to call them to God and put an end to the worship of false gods. Later, Prophet Muhammad PBUH concluded a marriage contract with Aishah, peace be upon her.

Prophet Muhammad's Night Journey and Ascension

In the twelfth year of Prophet Muhammad's mission, Angel Gabriel came down to Prophet Muhammad PBUH and opened his chest up again to remove his heart and wash it to strengthen him to what he was about to see and experience, known as the Night Journey and Ascension. Prophet Muhammad PBUH took a night journey from Masjid Al-Haram in Mecca to Masjid Al-Aqsa in Jerusalem on a speedy beast, which was pure white and called Al-Buraq, in the company of the Archangel Gabriel. When they reached their destination, they tied the beast to a ring in the gate of the Mosque. Prophet Muhammad PBUH prayed two units of prayer, turned around, and found all the Prophets behind him. He led the Prophets in Prayer.

After visiting Masjid Al-Aqsa, they ascended physically to the Heavens. Angel Gabriel set out with Prophet Muhammad PBUH on the same horse till they reached the first Heaven. When the gate opened, Prophet Muhammad PBUH saw Prophet Adam in the first Heaven. Angel Gabriel introduced Prophet Adam to Prophet Muhammad, peace be upon them both. Then Angel Gabriel and Prophet Muhammad ascended to the second Heaven, then the third, and then the fourth, fifth, sixth, and seventh, where they saw and greeted other Prophets of God, including Prophet John, and Jesus, Joseph, Enoch, and Aaron, Moses, and Abraham, peace be upon them all.

Then Prophet Muhammad PBUH was carried to the Remotest Lote-Tree where its fruits are like jugs, and its leaves are as big as elephant ears. He was also shown The Much-Frequented House, located above the Kaa'ba in the Seventh Heaven, where a group of 70,000 angels circle it, and never return being followed by the next group of 70,000 Angels and will continue like this until the Day of Judgment. Prophet Muhammad PBUH was then presented to the Divine Presence of Allah, the Glorious, where Allah issued the five daily prayers to us. When Prophet Muhammad PBUH returned, some people believed in his story, as they were well aware of the Power and Ability of God. Some did not believe him and mocked him, including one of the biggest enemies of Islam, Abu Jahl.

The Muslims Migrate to the City of Medina

Later, the people of Yathrib, who had spoken to Prophet Muhammad PBUH the year prior, had converted to Islam, returned to Prophet Muhammad, promising to support him, and invited him to their city, which Prophet Muhammad PBUH agreed to. Now that the Muslims had a place to live without persecution, many migrated to Yathrib, later named Medina. About one hundred families quietly migrated from Mecca to Medina secretly. Many Muslim immigrants who traveled to Abyssinia prior also migrated to Medina. The Prophet, his cousin Ali, and his friend Abu Bakr remained in Mecca for the time being. The Prophet PBUH was waiting for instructions from God before migrating.

The idol-worshippers of Mecca feared the growth and power of the Muslims. They saw them as a threat to their religion and began to think of ways to kill Prophet Muhammad PBUH even though that would go against their laws, as it was unheard of to kill someone of their own blood, especially in the sacred land of Mecca. Each tribe sent one of their young men to the Prophet's house to kill him. Then Angel Gabriel was sent down to Prophet Muhammad PBUH to tell him what the idol-worshippers of Mecca were plotting. Angel Gabriel also informed Prophet Muhammad PBUH that he had Allah's permission to leave Makkah. The enemies of the Prophet surrounded his house. However, Allah covered their eyes and blinded them, allowing Prophet Muhammad PBUH to escape while reciting Verses from Chapter Yaseen from the Holy Quran. Prophet Muhammad PBUH and his companion, Abu Bakr, fled to a cave named Thor, where they spent three days.

Upon arrival in Medina, Prophet Muhammad's first task was to build a Mosque called Masjid Quba on the same site where his camel had knelt. Prophet Muhammad PBUH helped his companions make this Mosque by carrying bricks and stones while reciting Verses of the Holy Quran. With God and the Holy Quran's Guidance, Prophet Muhammad PBUH taught and preached the Islamic way of life to his companions in Medina. He was their guide, teacher, judge, consoler, arbitrator, adviser, and father figure to the new community.

The migration of the Muslims to Medina is known as *'The Hijra'* in Arabic and was later chosen as the start of the Muslim calendar. Those who emigrated from Mecca to Medina earned the title of *Muhajireen (The Emigrants)*. The Muslims living in Medina welcomed and supported the emigrants and adopted the title *'The Ansar' (The Helpers)*. Prophet Muhammad PBUH made a pact of mutual religious solidarity between both Muslim groups.

Prophet Muhammad PBUH entered treaties with other tribes living around them that they would all support one another in defending the city against an attack. For the first time, the Muslims had their own state. After about a year and a half after the Muslims had migrated to Medina, the Qibla (the direction in which Muslims pray) was changed after Prophet Muhammad PBUH, made a dua (prayer supplication) to Allah, the Glorious, to change the direction from Masjid Al-Aqsa to the Kaaba.

The Battle of Badr—Supported by Angels

Towards the second year of the Muslims migrating to Medina, the idol-worshippers of Mecca began a series of harsh acts against the Muslims living in Medina. They sent men to destroy the Muslim's fruit trees and carry away their flocks. Soon, permission was given by God to Prophet Muhammad and the Muslims, peace be upon them, to fight back to protect themselves and their families because they had been wronged by the oppressive idol worshippers, who'd kicked them out of their homes in Mecca and denied them their basic freedoms and rights. Prophet Muhammad PBUH and the Muslims prepared their state military.

A force of 1,300 men of Mecca's idol worshippers marched under their leader Abu Jahl, the great enemy of Islam, toward Medina and the Muslims to attack them. Prophet Muhammad PBUH had sent scouts and learned their enemies were on their way to kill them.

About 313 Muslims gathered in the plains of Badr, located near the sea between Mecca and Medina, with only seventy camels and three horses. They had their men ride taking turns since they did not have enough. This battle is known as the Battle of Badr because it occurred in the Valley of Badr. The two armies met in the month of Ramadan. Prophet Muhammad PBUH, spent the whole night praying and supplicating to God, the Most Merciful, that his small Muslim army would not be destroyed. As the two armies met in the Valley of Badr, Allah, the Glorious, supported the Muslims with 1,000 angels that came down to fight alongside them. With the help of the angels, the Muslims could defeat the idol worshippers. The battle ended with the idol-worshippers of Mecca fleeing back to Mecca with a significant loss. Several of their chiefs and leaders were killed, including Abu Jahl. Seventy of the idol-worshippers of Mecca were dead, while only 15 Muslims died as martyrs from the Muslims. The idol-worshippers also had 70 of their people taken as prisoners of war, who remained in the hands of the Muslims.

The Battle of Uhud-- Muslims Archers Leave their Post

The Battle of Badr left Mecca's idol worshippers grieving from their loss, and they wanted to seek revenge against the Muslims. Later, another battle occurred between the idol-worshippers of Mecca and the Muslims, called the Battle of Uhud, a hill about four miles to the north of the city of Medina. The idol-worshippers made better preparations this time to attack the Muslims. The idol-worshippers gathered an army of 3,000 men, 200 horses, and even two dozen of their women under their current leader, Abu Sufyan. The Muslims were fewer at around 1,000 men and only one horse. Later, the Muslims were abandoned by 300 hypocrites of the Muslims, so the number of Muslims dripped to 700 men instead of 1,000.

Prophet Muhammad PBUH and the Muslims offered their prayers in the morning, then advanced to the plains to prepare for battle. When they reached the place of battle, Prophet Muhammad PBUH positioned some of his men with their backs toward the hill. Prophet Muhammad PBUH then placed fifty Muslim archers on top of the mountain behind the Muslim troops to prevent the idol-worshippers from surrounding the Muslims, so they could have a good view from afar. Prophet Muhammad PBUH commanded the Muslim archers on top of the hill not to leave their post no matter what happened, even if they saw the idol worshipers fleeing. He was very strict and precise about this.

Later, it seemed like the Muslims had defeated the idol-worshippers. On top of the hill, the Muslim archers saw that the idol-worshippers were fleeing the battlefield and had left some of their stuff behind. On top of the mountain, the Muslim archers began to dispute whether they should go down and grab what the idol-worshippers had left behind. The leader of the Muslim archers that Prophet Muhammad PBUH appointed asked, *'Have you forgotten what Prophet Muhammad PBUH told us?'*

Fifty Muslim archers who were instructed not to leave their post left their positions, except for ten. This allowed the idol-worshippers of Mecca to come back around, climb the hill, attack the Muslims, surround, and surprise them from the back, and create complete disorder, which resulted in the Muslims losing.

Prophet Muhammad PBUH called his companions back, but only twelve men remained with the Prophet PBUH. Prophet Muhamad PBUH was struck down by stones, wounded in the face by two arrows, and fell unconscious. About seventy or seventy-five of the Muslims were killed in this battle; among them was the Prophet's uncle Hamza, peace be upon them all. Of the idol worshippers, twenty-two men died.

The Betrayal of the Jewish Tribes of Medina

After the Muslims lost the Battle of Uhud, the Muslims were treated differently by the Jewish and Arab tribes in Medina. The Jewish tribe of Banu Qaynuqa increased their hostility against the Muslims. They told Prophet Muhammad PBUH when he came to remind them of their treaty not to be deceived over their victory in the Battle of Badr against the idol-worshippers of Quraish since they had little understanding of the art of war. They added if the Muslims had fought them, they would see how war really was and how fierce an enemy they were. They also broke the Muslim treaty by killing a Muslim in the marketplace. So, Prophet Muhammad PBUH ended the treaty with them and expelled them from the city by giving them three days to pack their stuff and leave.

Another Jewish tribe in Medina called Bani Nadhir also broke their treaty with the Muslims by attempting to kill Prophet Muhammad PBUH, by asking him to sit in a particular place where they tried to drop a big piece of a wall of a fortress. But Angel Gabriel told Prophet Muhammad PBUH what they were plotting, and he got up. Prophet Muhammad PBUH had no choice but to expel this Jewish tribe from Medina for their evil actions and betrayal. Prophet Muhammad PBUH asked them to grab all their belongings and leave the city, which they did and moved to a neighboring town named Khaybar.

The Battle of the Trench

Soon, the Jewish tribe of Bani Nadhir that were expelled from their homes because of what they had done to the Muslims wanted to get back the land they'd lost and wipe out the Muslims. They started to recruit and negotiate alliances with other tribes, including the idol-worshippers of Mecca. They also dealt with the hypocrites of the Muslims to help them attack them. In the fifth year of the Muslims migrating to Medina, Abu Sufyan, the leader of the idol-worshippers at the time, set out with 10,000 men from different tribes. This was the greatest army ever seen in the Arabian Peninsula at the time. The Muslims only had about 2,500-3,000 men, so they were vastly outnumbered again. This battle was called the *Battle of Al-Ahzab (The Battle of the Confederates or Groups)*.

The Muslims needed a plan to defend themselves against the enemies of Islam. One of the companions, Salman the Persian, PBUH, suggested digging a deep ditch around the city, making it difficult for the enemies to cross over quickly. Digging a trench was a technique used by the Persians, and it was unheard of by the Arabs. They did not need to dig through the entire city since part of the city of Medina was covered with volcanic rock formations, mountains, and houses tightly congested together. Large plantations of date trees made it impossible for large armies to get through.

All the Muslims, including Prophet Muhammad and children, peace be upon them, worked together to dig the trenches, using only a shovel. The trench was about thirteen feet wide and two kilometers long and took around 1-to 2 weeks to dig. Once the trench had been dug, they waited for the enemies to come. When they arrived, the enemies of Islam saw the ditch and were surprised. The enemies of Islam realized they would not be able to jump past the ditch with their animals because of its width, and they would not be able to climb down the ditch with their animals either. They would have to go down the ditch individually, putting themselves at risk of easily getting hit by the Muslims as they climbed down.

The enemies of Islam camped outside the trenches in tents to discuss their next move. Then the enemies decided to send someone to the Jewish tribe living inside Medina and ask them to join and help them attack the Muslims from inside. The Jewish tribe living inside initially refused at first because of their treaty with the Muslims. But after being tempted, they agreed to join the enemies and attack the Muslims from the inside while others attacked the Muslims from the outside.

Once the Muslims heard the Jewish tribe from inside had betrayed them, they panicked and were terrified as they were about to be attacked from inside and outside the city. Prophet Muhammad PBUH sent all the women and kids to the home of one of the companions, a blind person. Then God the Almighty sent down strong winds, a sandstorm, which had never hit the city of Medina like this before. The enemy's pots of food were blown and spilled all over, making it very difficult to see anything. The enemies had no other choice but to flee, which they did, and they were defeated without a war. The Muslims then eliminated the Jewish tribe of Banu Qurayza that betrayed the Muslims living inside the city of Medina.

The Treaty of Hudaybiyyah

Prophet Muhammad PBUH had a dream of entering Makkah unopposed, doing tawaf (circling the Kaaba) in ihram, and shaving his hair. He interpreted this dream to mean he would be performing Umrah (a lesser pilgrimage) in Mecca with his 1,400 companions, peace be upon them.

Prophet Muhammad and his companions, peace be upon them, traveled to perform Umrah; and as they drew near, they were warned that the idol-worshippers of Quraish had sworn to prevent Prophet Muhammad and the Muslims from entering Makkah. God the Almighty caused the Prophet's camel to camp at a plain called, Hudaybiyyah.

After Prophet Muhammad PBUH and the idol worshippers sent people back and forth to talk on their behalf, they met in person. Prophet Muhammad PBUH explained to the idol-worshippers of Quraish that they had only come to perform pilgrimage and had no intentions of fighting. After negotiating back and forth, the truce of Hudaybiyyah was signed by both groups. The treaty between the Muslims and the idol worshippers of Quraish in Mecca stated that there would be no fighting between the two parties for ten years. No side would be allowed to attack the other side, including the tribes that had joined the treaty. And if any other tribe in Arabia wished to join the Muslims or idol-worshippers of Quraish, they could do so.

Prophet Muhammad's companions did not like the treaty's terms, as they seemed unfavorable to them. Yet the Prophet PBUH accepted, honored, and abided by the treaty. During the return journey from Hudaybiyyah, God the Almighty revealed a Chapter in the Holy Quran named '*Al-Fath (The Victory).*' God revealed that this truce was indeed a great victory for the Muslims. With this new treaty, the religion of Islam was able to flourish in the Arabian Peninsula and spread rapidly. The Muslims went from having 1,400 men in this gathering to 10,000 men two years later to liberate Makkah. A lot of good happened two years after this treaty was signed.

The Conquest of Makkah

Over the next year or two, different surrounding tribes joined either the Muslim's side or the side of the idol-worshippers of Mecca. One of the tribes that joined the idol-worshippers side was the Tribe of Bakr, and one of the tribes that joined the Muslim side was the Tribe of Banu Khuzaʻah. Both tribes did not like each other and had a history of fighting.

The Tribe of Bakr, from the idol-worshippers side, asked permission from the Meccan idol-worshippers if they could attack and confiscate the belongings of the Tribe of Khuzaʻah from the Muslim side, even though that would go against the treaty that was signed. The idol-worshippers of Mecca allowed it and even provided them with weapons to earn a share of the profits they were going to confiscate and advised them to go at night so they wouldn't be seen.

After the attack, the news reached Prophet Muhammad and the Muslims, peace be upon them. The idol-worshippers got nervous and decided to send their leader, Abu Sufyan, to talk to Prophet Muhammad PBUH, and ask for the existing treaty to be renewed. However, Prophet Muhammad PBUH did not assure him that the treaty was still valid because they had broken it.

After this event, Prophet Muhammad PBUH and the Muslims raised an enormous army of 10,000 men to surprise attack the idol worshippers in Mecca for what they did. When the Muslims reached Mecca, the people were overwhelmed and unable to fight the Muslims. Prophet Muhammad PBUH did not fight them and offered safety and security to anyone that did not resist. He announced to the people of Mecca that anyone who stayed in the Kaaba, their homes, or in the house of Abu Sufiyan—their leader who ended up converting to Islam —would be safe.

Prophet Muhammad PBUH entered Mecca with his head bowed in humility, his head touching the back of his camel. He also circulated the Kaaba. This was the end of many years of persecution. Prophet Muhammad and the Muslims, peace be upon them, conquered the city of Mecca in a bloodless battle.

Then he ordered every idol in Kaaba to be destroyed and participated in destroying all 360 idols. Prophet Muhammad PBUH would point at an idol, and it would fall to the ground. The Kaaba was purified of all idols. Prophet Muhammad PBUH then ordered Bilal, who had a strong melodious voice, to call the Adhan, which became the first Adhan in Islamic history from the Kaaba, proclaiming the worship of the one the only true God.

The Farewell Hajj

After Makkah had been conquered, Prophet Muhamad and many of his companions, peace be upon them, returned to Medina. It was the 9th year of the Hijrah. Prophet Muhammad and his companions, peace be upon them, hosted groups of representatives of different tribes in the Prophet's Mosque in Medina. Each tribe from the Arabian Peninsula sent a group of representatives to greet Prophet Muhammad PBUH to declare their allegiance and pledge their commitment to him. The representatives of each tribe heard the Holy Quran being recited, watched the companions pray, and learned about Islam from Prophet Muhamad PBUH. The representatives of the tribes returned to their people, calling them to accept Islam, teaching them what they'd learned, and telling them they needed to get rid of all their idols.

Eventually, the whole Arabian Peninsula accepted Islam. In the 10th year of the Hijrah, Allah, the Glorious, revealed a command to perform Hajj for those capable of doing so. Prophet Muhammad PBUH announced that he was going to perform Hajj Pilgrimage to Mecca. Flocks of people—tens of thousands from all over—joined him. It was the largest gathering in the Arabian Peninsula at the time.

Throughout the Hajj pilgrimage, Prophet Muhammad PBUH gave several sermons, including the famous primary speech on the day of Arafat from the plain of Arafat (Mount of Mercy). There, he declared equality and solidarity between all the Muslims and reminded them of all the duties Islam had enjoined upon them. He forbade racism, stealing, killing people, involvement in interest, and more. He commanded everyone to be good and just to their wives and other women.

He told them there were two things to hold on to so they would not go astray: the Book of Allah, which is the Holy Quran, and the Sunnah which is the teachings of the last and final Prophet, Muhammad PBUH. He reminded them that they would return to their Lord one day, who would judge them based on their deeds. In the end, he asked them, *'Have I not conveyed the Message?'* The companions replied, *'Yes!'* Then Prophet Muhammad PBUH raised his hands in the air, looked up into the sky, and said three times, *'O Allah, you bear witness!'*

Prophet Muhammad Returns to Medina & Passes Away

Prophet Muhammad PBUH received his final Revelation from God. Now that the faith of Islam was well established among his people and his community, his mission was coming to an end. Soon after, Prophet Muhammad PBUH returned to the city of Medina.

Soon after that, Prophet Muhammad PBUH, fell ill for 10 to 12 days as his fever worsened in the house of his wife, Aisha, peace be upon her, the mother of the believers. His body would get hot, and Aisha, peace be upon her, would recite the Holy Quran over him and cool him off with a wet towel.

He sadly passed away on the lap of his wife, Aisha, peace be upon her. His companions were in shock and very sad about this tragedy. He was buried in the exact place where he died, and his companions prayed for him individually.

Today, millions of Muslims go to Medina and send their salutations to our blessed Prophet PBUH. In the Holy Quran, God states that He did not send Prophet Muhammad PBUH, except as a mercy for humanity. His role as the leader of the Islamic State was taken over by Abu Bakr, peace be upon him.

The End.

Made in the USA
Middletown, DE
05 November 2023

41951074R00024